IT'S TIME TO EAT CHICKEN AND WAFFLES

It's Time to Eat CHICKEN AND WAFFLES

Walter the Educator

Silent King Books
A WhichHead Entertainment Imprint

Disclaimer

This book is a literary work; the story is not about specific persons, locations, situations, and/or circumstances unless mentioned in a historical context. Any resemblance to real persons, locations, situations, and/or circumstances is coincidental. This book is for entertainment and informational purposes only. The author and publisher offer this information without warranties expressed or implied. No matter the grounds, neither the author nor the publisher will be accountable for any losses, injuries, or other damages caused by the reader's use of this book. The use of this book acknowledges an understanding and acceptance of this disclaimer.

It's Time to Eat CHICKEN AND WAFFLES is a collectible early learning book by Walter the Educator suitable for all ages belonging to Walter the Educator's Time to Eat Book Series. Collect more books at WaltertheEducator.com

USE THE EXTRA SPACE TO TAKE NOTES AND DOCUMENT YOUR MEMORIES

CHICKEN AND WAFFLES

It's time to eat, so take a seat,

It's Time to Eat

Chicken

and

Waffles

Chicken and waffles, what a treat!

Crispy, golden, and fluffy, too,

A yummy meal just made for you!

Start with the waffle, warm and round,

With tiny squares where syrup is found.

Soft on the inside, crunchy outside,

A cozy hug for taste buds to ride.

Next comes the chicken, fried so nice,

A crispy crust, a little spice.

Juicy and tender, it's quite the pair,

With waffles waiting right under there.

Drizzle the syrup, sweet and slow,

Over the chicken and waffles below.

Golden rivers that shimmer and shine,

Oh, this dinner is truly divine!

It's Time to Eat

Chicken

and

Waffles

Add a dollop of butter, creamy and light,

Melting slowly, it's such a sight!

It glides on the waffle and makes it glow,

A swirl of magic with every flow.

Pick up your fork and take a bite,

The flavors blend, it feels so right!

Savory chicken and syrup so sweet,

Together they're a perfect treat.

Crunch, munch, and give a cheer,

Your favorite meal is finally here.

Each tasty bite feels like a song,

Chicken and waffles can't go wrong!

We share and laugh as we eat away,

This meal makes for the best of days.

Friends and family gather 'round,

It's Time to Eat

Chicken and Waffles

With every plate, love can be found.

So if you're hungry, don't delay,

Chicken and waffles save the day!

Let's dig in, it's time to feast,

The best of both, to say the least!

When the meal is done, we'll smile so wide,

Our hearts are full and warm inside.

Chicken and waffles, a tasty delight,

It's Time to Eat

Chicken

and

Waffles

The perfect dish, morning or night!

ABOUT THE CREATOR

Walter the Educator is one of the pseudonyms for Walter Anderson. Formally educated in Chemistry, Business, and Education, he is an educator, an author, a diverse entrepreneur, and he is the son of a disabled war veteran. "Walter the Educator" shares his time between educating and creating. He holds interests and owns several creative projects that entertain, enlighten, enhance, and educate, hoping to inspire and motivate you. Follow, find new works, and stay up to date with Walter the Educator™

at WaltertheEducator.com